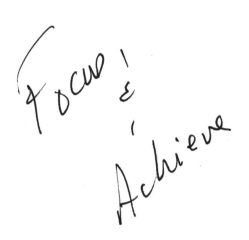

*Focus &
Achieve*

Achieving Strategic Alignment

2nd Edition

Barry

Reviews for "Achieving Strategic Alignment"

Communicating multiple objectives through multiple business segments while at the same time growing our business was a challenge our company was facing, and quite honestly was struggling with. Barry's process allowed us to take a logical process of accountability and buy-in and combine it with clear, concise, and effective communication to realize results in our company we never thought possible. In addition, the pulse and the enthusiasm within our management group was noticeably upbeat and positive, and months later the energy is still there along with better bottom-line results!

Jay England, CEO, Pride Transport, Inc.

What a beneficial and timely book. It came to me at just the right time, giving me the direction and the strategy our company needed. This book guided our management team as we designed and implemented our successful succession plan.

What a great resource for any management team.

H. Austin Kravik, CEO, E F Bailey Company

Barry's book is a must read for CEOs and those who counsel them. The thorough approach and emphasis on *alignment,* not just planning, is incredibly timely and valuable. Too many planning sessions and strategic plans are quickly shelved, only to gather dust. Here is a practical, workable approach that ensures the leader can drive into the company parking lot knowing everyone inside the building is aligned with the organization's strategic vision.

Scott Seagren, CPCC, ORSCC,
PCC, Vistage International-Chicago, IL

Mr. MacKechnie provides a comprehensive, easy-to-understand roadmap for creating and executing a meaningful Strategic Plan. The structure of his book provides bite-sized, well-described descriptions of what an organization must do to achieve strategic alignment. Finally, there is a book that enables CEOs to quickly and efficiently create then implement a strategic plan!

David R. Lazzara, Vistage International, California

It is strategic! It is pragmatic! It works! And it is easy to share with your team.

Stephane Bennour, CEO, NEOS-SDI, USA, France

This book is a perfect tool for companies looking to create and execute their strategic plans. It provides a very simple and concise way for setting a strategic plan and actually achieving it!

Tuanhai Hoang, President, Qualitel Corporation

The information in the book is a simple easy to follow step by step process to get your team thinking strategically and achieving alignment. We held an off-site strategic planning session based on Barry's principles. Our team initially started off very conservative when we began budgeting for the year (I think we had self-limiting beliefs). After considering our total market and reconsidering our budget, we budgeted for 35% growth (up from 5% originally) and put the pieces in place to make it happened. We are accomplishing growth of 45% in revenue this year. This is following 59% growth last year.

We have trained in advance to have the capability, hired to have the capacity and changed our organizational chart based on the principles in this book. Achieving Strategic Alignment is a short read with simple well organized principles that really work.

Don O. Nelson – President, Nelson and Sons Construction Co. Inc.

Barry MacKechnie has unique insights into leadership dynamics that as an author enables him to bring clear focus to creating and achieving corporate strategy in his book "Achieving Strategic Alignment". His experience as an effective strategic planning session facilitator is demonstrated by how his framework turns a very complex process into a set of clearly defined steps that lead to an organization breaking its financial barriers.

Doug Ostrom, President, Stafford Health Services, Inc.

I am Co-Founder and CEO of a marketing technology startup bringing disruptive innovations to two industries. Barry's book and facilitation have been invaluable in helping my team simplify the complex. Barry's roadmap has helped us define a solid strategy with transparent tactics.

Matt Furry, CEO, SingUlarity

Mr. MacKechnie has successfully created an easy-read blueprint for achieving strategic alignment and strategic planning with certain ROI. Keeping the concepts simple and delivered in a sequential manner make this book a useful "how to" resource for any CEO seeking strategic alignment.

Eric Overton, CEO, Sparling

Barry's book provides a most useful description of the process of organizational strategic thinking and its application to your unique business situation. Mr. MacKechnie's straight forward and practical approach will be used to help us provide that critical alignment in our small organization

Robert S. Eaton, Founder and Managing Member, Eaton Hotel Investments

Barry MacKechnie's book gives a very consistent and structured approach to the whole strategic alignment thinking. Most CEOs have probably heard here and there some of the things he is describing. But with the help of his book one gets a concrete guideline how to run the process of strategic alignment step by step. It is easy to read and has great examples. And it is only approximately 100 pages, meaning it focuses the reader on the relevant things without any distracting theories that do not help in real life.

Dick Lueth

Mr. MacKechnie's book is a concise and comprehensive tool that provides real world descriptions of how organizations can become strategically aligned. The book is an easy read with concise chapters and real world examples leading CEOs to the holy grail of strategic alignment.

James T. Peterson, Vistage
International, San Ramon, CA

Mr. MacKechnie has successfully created an easy-read blueprint for achieving strategic alignment. Keeping the concepts simple and delivered in a sequential manner make this book a useful "how to" resource for any business seeking strategic alignment.

Joe Stanik, VP Finance, Cashmere Molding, Inc.

This is a great book for CEO's - it is concise, to the point and full of great info. It is ideal for helping CEOs build alignment and to develop a cohesive plan with their team's involvement. The best leaders are servant leaders who trust their team to get the job done and empower them to do so. This book will help you do exactly that.

Richard Walker, CEO Efficient Technology, Inc.,
Author of "It's My Life! I Can Change If I Want To"

Great book! As a Small Business Owner I found this book to be an excellent resource in focusing my team. A "must-read" for CEO's.

Mr. MacKechnie's book continues to be a valuable resource for me and our organization. We are experiencing positive results from our strategic plan and related deliverables.

Chris E. Wallace, President/CEO, Greater Irving-Las Colinas Chamber of Commerce

Mr. MacKechnie provides a comprehensive, easy-to-understand roadmap for creating and executing a meaningful, differentiated Strategic Plan. The structure of his book provides bite-sized, well-described descriptions of what an organization must do to achieve stratetic alignment. As a successful business leader who has led a number of strategic planning sessions, I found Mr. MacKechnie's book to be complete, correct, and concise. It is a valuable guide, and I recommend it to all who want to maximize the success of their strategy planning and implementation.

Mike Redmond, President, Ops Savvy

In just a few hours you learn a lot about achieving strategic alignment. Here's a book that makes it possible for executive teams to learn how to create what they need most to execute their strategy: strategic alignment. Many of you reading this should have read this book long ago, but it wasn't written yet. Now it is. Read it from cover to cover. It takes just a few hours! Even if English isn`t a language you use on a daily basis (I`m Dutch). Reading this is just the first step in a process, but at least then you`ve started this process of gaining knowledge and experience. It starts with some knowledge based on the author's long-time experience and this is easily the quickest way to get access to this. It ends with results.

Rene van Dinten, Lecturer of (strategic) marketing & strategic performance management at Hogeschool Utrecht, Lecturer of (strategic) marketing & strategic performance management at University of applied sciences Utrecht, Netherlands

Useful the first day! This book gives you step-by-step techniques you can apply today. Not the usual 30,000 foot view that your company will get lost in.

Amazon.com reader review

Quick & easy read, packed with practical application. It has great step by step direction, great how-to tips and strong methodologies to get the entire organization in to lock step. I look forward to working these into my organization!

Rodney W. Ferris, CEO, F/T Construction

I thought this book was terrific, I run a small but dynamic company and getting all focused and moving the same direction is a huge challenge for us. We will apply what has been learned from this book.

Amazon.com reader review

A no nonsense inspirational read and a prerequisite for Senior Executives and current CEO's. Other authors should take note. I must say, "Very well done Barry".

Michael Ness, Director, Business Continuity at Virginia Mason Medical Center

Barry's book is an easy read with great content. It has excellent tips and insights with wonderful templates. A must read for CEO's.

Business Development Coach, Amazon.com review

MacKechnie takes the typical business retreat to a new level with his book, Achieving Strategic Alignment. Getting buy-in at every level - not just at the top - improves the overall performance of a company. I can't wait to give it a try at our next retreat!

Tom Hoban, CEO, Coast Group

Barry has taken a subject that most entrepreneurs and CEO's downplay and shown both the importance of using these key processes to achieve even greater company results, as well as how easy the process can be if a systematic methodology is followed. And, he spells out that methodology in easy-to-understand terms.

Tom Englander, President, ES Interims

I suggest you buy a quick read, Achieving Strategic Alignment by Barry MacKechnie. The book, which can be read in two hours (three for me), not only discussed strategy, but gave a play by play approach to tactics. In other words, the book illustrated how to break down your journey to baby steps. We are overwhelmed with knowledge on a daily basis. Any tool, like this book, that can streamline your learning process and still present results, leverages your time efficiently, and will bring returns for years to come.

The L.A. CPA

What a great find. Whether you're in the Strategy or consulting business or play a leadership roll in your organization, Achieving Strategic Alignment is the perfect read. 1. it's only a 100 pages or so, 2. it lays out everything you need to keep in mind when it comes to rolling up your sleeves and doing the tough work of a re-org, re-brand, or a re-position and 3. I've never seen a book that keeps everyone involved, accountable for their actions. Most people leave half day or two days sessions, pumped for just a few weeks, then they run back to their corners and back to 'work'. This book keeps everyone at the table accountable for change through goal setting and follow-through. This is the perfect business book.

Ken Grant, Media Advisor, Motivated Branding

2nd Edition - Revised and Expanded

A Leadership and Results Blueprint for Executives
Changing How Your Organization Works

ACHIEVING STRATEGIC ALIGNMENT

HOW TO HARNESS ITS POWER TO EXCEED YOUR ORGANIZATIONAL GOALS

BARRY MACKECHNIE

DoubleBee Publishing

DoubleBee Publishing, Inc.

17910 SE 106th Street

Renton, WA 98059

International Standard Book Numbers

Soft Cover: 978-1-4392-7422-4

Hard Cover: 978-1-4392-7229-9

eBook: 978-1-4507-3966-5

Printed in the United States of America

Library of Congress Cataloging-in-Publication Data

MacKechnie, Barry

Achieving Strategic Alignment: Vol. 1 by Barry MacKechnie C.2010. ISBN: 978-1-4507-3567-4 LCCN: 2010936596

DEDICATION

To my wife Bette who has been the soul of my life and who has been by my side during every step of my professional career as I gained my experience and channeled it into this book. Without her love and support, I would not have accomplished what I have achieved in my life.

Be mine forever.

I am forever yours.

ABOUT THE AUTHOR

Barry MacKechnie has more than 45 years of experience as a business leader, working with CEO's in over 450 businesses and as a business owner and CEO himself. Based upon his extensive business experience, Barry has developed a blueprint for executives to follow as they lead their organization through the process of achieving strategic alignment. Barry facilitates strategic planning sessions for organizations across the spectrum of industries and performs CEO workshops on achieving strategic alignment throughout the United States. Barry is an exciting public speaker on transforming the way businesses work to meet and exceed organizational goals.

Contact Information:
Barry MacKechnie
17910 SE 106th Street
Newcastle, WA 98059
Email: barry@ceo-services.com
Phone: 206-399-5698
Website: www.ceo-services.com
Blog: http://www.ceo-services.com/barrysblog

TABLE OF CONTENTS

WHY I DECIDED TO PUBLISH A REVISED VERSION OF THE BOOK

In the two years since I published the first edition of **Achieving Strategic Alignment**, I have spent over 3,000 hours leading CEO workshops, delivering speeches to hundreds of CEOs and working with a variety of organizations across the United States. During that time, I have introduced new tools to enhance the capability of an organization to drive the achievement of its goals down through the entire organization. I have worked with several executive teams and their direct reports to improve their ability to set achievable goals. I accomplished this by introducing them to two new tools; creative brainstorming and mind mapping. By strengthening the capability to brainstorm more creatively, organizations were able to explore outside of their normal business beliefs and stretch beyond their expectations. Using a tool called "mind-mapping" I was able to help businesses get their teams involved in the creation and delegation of action items which, when completed, would lead the organization to achieving its strategic plan goals. In this edition, I have added content to several chapters and written two new chapters: one on effective brainstorming and one on mind mapping. The goal of the new content is to provide every organization with new ways to explore capabilities and discover the ability to look beyond preconceived notions about what it is possible when you eliminate self-limiting beliefs.

I have added some examples of how organizations have used the content of this book to achieve their goals through better strategic alignment of their activities. As with the first book, my goal is that the 2nd Edition will provide every organization with a framework for setting strategic goals and "Achieving Strategic Alignment" in order to realize those goals.

INTRODUCTION

During my work with CEOs and their executive teams, I have watched amazing transformations in organizations as they take ownership of strategic alignment and begin to harness the powerful force that it generates. When an organization gains clarity on its goals and every employee understands how they can contribute to achieving those goals, the organization flourishes.

This book is a blueprint for you to follow as you go through the process of achieving strategic alignment in your organization. My book is not about the theory of strategic alignment. It is about how to achieve strategic alignment. Over the past forty-five years, I developed my approach to achieving strategic alignment by drawing from the experience and knowledge that I gained while working as a CEO and business owner as well as working with over 450 CEOs and business leaders.

I have purposefully kept my book short. To me, the most valuable business books are the ones that keep their message clear and concise. My goal was to pack it full of powerful information and tools but also ensure that it is a quick and engaging read. Ultimately, this book is meant to be read not once but re-read and referenced often as you move beyond theory to truly transformative application of the process of achieving strategic alignment.

In keeping with my commitment to my readers for clear and concise content, let's begin the process of achieving strategic alignment and actualizing the goals you set for your organization!

CHAPTER 1:
STRATEGIC ALIGNMENT

> ➤ Strategic Alignment
> ➤ Exposed Accountability
> ➤ Managing the Change
> ➤ Leadership to Strategic Alignment

Imagine what it will be like to go into your office and know that every employee in your organization is working on two or three focused deliverable tasks that, when completed, will help you achieve your strategic goals. Picture what you can accomplish as an organization where 100 percent of your employees consistently help drive your organization toward successfully reaching its goals. That is the power of strategic alignment. This book is about how to create, generate, and harness that power.

Strategic Alignment
This is not another book about teamwork, commitment, vision, and mission. Nowhere in this book will you find the all too familiar picture of four people in a row boat with the word "teamwork" emblazoned beneath it. I see a lot of strategy books available at the bookstore that talk about theory but they seldom give you a practical guide on how you can make their theory work in your organization.

What you will find in this book is a functional blueprint for creating strategic alignment along with detailed steps that you, your executive team, and your employees need to take to clarify the long and short term goals of your company in order to drive strategic alignment down through your entire organization.

Most strategic plans begin to fail within two weeks of creation. Let that sink in for a minute. They start failing within two weeks! How is that possible? The entire executive team was out of the office, locked away in a hotel conference room for two days working on a budget and plans for the upcoming year. How can the plan begin to fail within two weeks? The demise begins when the executive team returns from its planning retreat without a clearly defined plan for communicating the strategic goals to the rest of the organization. Likewise, there is no plan in place for getting the rest of the organization committed to the achievement of those goals. Strategic alignment does not trickle down through an organization. It is driven down through the organization by your commitment and your leadership. Without a focused effort to drive alignment down through an organization, a newly created strategic plan usually gets stuffed in a file cabinet where it will gather dust until it is opened again just before next year's strategy session.

Even more compelling is the fact that many strategic planning retreats miss the mark completely. I've had a few CEOs tell me about previous planning sessions where they spent two days developing company vision and mission statements. Don't misunderstand me—a mission and vision for your company are important, but they should not be something that you create during a strategic planning retreat. Your strategic planning session needs to be dedicated to you and your executive team understanding your industry, how you compete, creating realistic goals, and determining what it will take for your organization to achieve those goals.

Strategic alignment is not a theory. It happens when every member of an organization understand the strategic goals, the relevancy of each goal, and how each member plays a pivotal role in allowing the company to reach or exceed its organizational goals.

Complete the process of achieving strategic alignment and the goals of your strategic plan will be achieved.

Exposed Accountability

One of the important outcomes of achieving strategic alignment is what I call exposed accountability. Exposed accountability occurs when every employee is responsible for the achievement of two to three clearly defined deliverable goals. Each employee's deliverable goals are tracked in order to manage their progress and to hold them accountable for successfully reaching their deliverable goals in a timely manner. Exposed accountability helps you identify your organization's areas of strength and weakness. Some of your employees will exceed your expectations because they thrive in a goal oriented organization. Other employees will show their weakness for managing change or for staying focused on the delivery of their two to three goals. I cover this in greater detail in chapter 8, but it is important to note that achieving strategic alignment requires exposed accountability.

Managing the Change

Becoming strategically aligned requires a change of culture because it exposes everyone in the organization to being held accountable for the delivery of their individual action items. You and your executive team will be required to provide consistent and collaborative leadership in order to successfully achieve strategic alignment.

I know that the words "culture change" can put fear in the minds of most business leaders. Achieving strategic alignment requires that everyone in your organization become aware of the necessity to achieve your goals and the role that each of them plays in that task. In most organizations, this requires a change in the way that employees think about their daily efforts. Strategic alignment usually requires a modification in the culture of an organization. Guiding your organization through the shift to strategic alignment requires strong leadership. As the leader of your team of executives, you must be clear and consistent about your commitment in order to successfully reach your strategic goals. Every member of your executive team needs to exemplify that commitment and reiterate it to the rest of the organization.

Strategic alignment changes the way your organization works. The change starts by setting and communicating clearly defined goals to your entire organization. You and your leadership team will then work with every employee to focus their efforts on achieving their goals. You keep the progress being made toward achieving goals front and center in every meeting with teams and individual employees by continually checking on the status of everyone's efforts. This requires hard, focused work from you and your executive team to make sure that everyone stays on track. Continual tracking will lead individuals, teams, and, ultimately, your entire organization to meet or exceed your organizational goals. Strategic alignment is a commitment that requires full participation from everyone in your organization. That focused drive for success from 100 percent of your employees will forever change the way your organization works.

Leadership
I worked with one member of an executive team who was not making progress toward reaching her goals and was a distraction to the rest of the executive team. The CEO in that company first tried to coach the individual and, when this failed, made the decision to remove that person from the executive team. The impact on the rest of the executive team was positive in many ways. The CEO had demonstrated the type of leadership that he expected from the entire executive team. At the same time, he showed the entire company his absolute commitment to achieving strategic alignment and reaching the company's strategic goals.

Your leadership throughout the process of achieving strategic alignment is critical. Consistent and committed leadership from you will create an environment of excitement and focus as everyone in your organization feels the growing power of strategic alignment.

Selecting a planning session facilitator
Most CEOs realize that they cannot or should not facilitate their strategic planning retreat. The CEO should be a

participant, not the facilitator, and it is almost impossible to wear both hats at the same time. Choosing the right facilitator is the first step you will take toward achieving strategic alignment. A great facilitator will focus on the process of your strategic planning session. They will ensure that everyone participates, agenda items are completed, and discussions are focused on creating and defining realistic goals. A facilitator is impartial and objective. Selecting and hiring the right strategic planning session facilitator is one of the most important decisions you will make as you begin planning your retreat. First and foremost, you need to make sure that your facilitator has a broad spectrum of business experience. They must have seen hundreds of different organizations both for-profit and not-for-profit. They must be excellent communicators so that they can easily guide you and your executive team through your strategic planning session. Your facilitator needs to have experience in guiding teams through a goal setting process and through the process of testing the reality and achievability of each of your strategic goals. He or she must have the ability to get dialogues started, keep a dialogue flowing and focused on its goals, and to make certain that all of your strategic planning retreat attendees are involved in the conversation. A good strategic planning facilitator knows when to intervene in a discussion in order to keep it on subject and tracking toward a logical conclusion. Your facilitator should be an unobtrusive force who guides your session but does not affect your decisions. One of my past clients gave the best description of a facilitator: "We hired you because we thought you had all of the answers. What we discovered during the retreat was that we had all of the answers but it took your guidance to help us find them."

You should select a strategic planning session facilitator before you begin the preparatory work that is detailed in chapter 2. Many of the items covered in preparing for your strategic planning retreat can be completed by your planning session facilitator. Your facilitator should be present at all of the pre-retreat planning meetings which are covered in the next chapter.

A good facilitator acts as the objective observer in the room, questioning the goals and expectations set by the company in order to reveal any self-limiting beliefs. Organizations tend to think about growing and changing their business based upon their own internal experience. As a planning facilitator, it is my responsibility to ask questions about every goal.

One of my clients went through the initial steps of setting their goals for 1, 3 and 5 years into the future. I questioned their revenue targets, initiating a discussion that revealed their goals were lower than the industry's growth rate estimates. They would, in fact, lose market share if they accepted their first set of goals. As I led them through the discussion, I asked them why they had set their targets so low. Their response was that they didn't think they could ever be that large of a company. That is a self-limiting belief.

Most organizations will set goals that are too low because they do not know how to achieve higher goals. By exposing self-limiting beliefs, a facilitator can assist you and your team through the discussion about how to eliminate any self-limiting beliefs and what changes your organization may need to make in order to achieve higher goals.

Commit yourself and your team to the process of achieving strategic alignment and you will be continually surprised by your organization's ability to consistently exceed its goals.

Strategic alignment is a process that begins with choosing a facilitator, doing your pre-retreat work, completing the actual retreat itself, and following through with post-retreat work that drives the goals you have established through your entire company. My book outlines each critical step along this path.

NOTES:

CHAPTER 2: PREPARING FOR THE STRATEGIC PLANNING SESSION

- ➢ The goals of a strategic planning session
  - ○ Six critical elements of a successful strategic planning session
    - ▪ Define your expected outcome
    - ▪ Pre-planning session meeting with your executive team
    - ▪ Complete pre-planning session groundwork
    - ▪ Create an agenda
    - ▪ Mandate participation
    - ▪ Set expectations for clearly defined results

The work product of your strategic planning session is the blueprint that will guide your company's efforts as you achieve your strategic goals. Long-range plans are vital for sustained growth because they define and align common objectives, goals, and results. In the next three chapters, you will learn about the advance preparation you need to complete to ensure a great strategic planning retreat.

The best strategic plans are made when you and your executive team can devote one to two days to the task away from the daily distractions at your office. You and your team will be setting in motion a process that will convert your company into a strategically aligned organization where 100 percent of your employees will know they are making a direct contribution to the company reaching its goals. That takes dedication and focused concentration. If you want to have some team building programs or some opportunities for your team to bond with each other, do that after you have completed your strategic planning retreat. Having a successful strategic planning session requires hard work and clear heads. Your team needs to be fresh and rested in order to maximize your one to two day planning session.

A great strategic planning session requires an atmosphere of open dialogue with a free exchange of ideas within an environment of creativity and common goal setting. To create this, there should be no distractions. In the planning retreats I have facilitated I tell the attendees that they must turn off their cell phones and PDAs. I make sure that there are several breaks of sufficient duration during the day to allow people to make phone calls and check emails. I often find that as the planning session progresses fewer and fewer attendees spend their breaks returning phone calls or clearing emails. A great strategic planning retreat builds momentum, excitement, and captures the attention of the participants so much that they want to get back quickly to the session without any distractions.

Your strategic planning retreat should include all of your key executives. If you were to look at an organization chart this would include such positions as your Chief Financial Officer, Chief Information Officer, Chief Operations Officer, Directors of Sales, Marketing, and Human Resources. The list should be limited to those people that help you manage your business on a day-to-day basis. These are the people that will be held accountable for driving the achievement of your company's strategic goals down through your organization. They are your key managers.

Today, more business leaders are inviting the key employees that report directly to the executive team into the strategic planning sessions. This gets more of the managers into the process of setting the goals of the organization. The best format for this type of additional management involvement is to have the executive team meet for a full day to set goals, review competition, examine industry trends and identify some deliverable action items. The second full day should involve the key people who report directly to the executive team. These key people go through the same process that the executive team completed during their full day. The key people review the competition, examine industry trends and complete a goal setting process. They also create deliverable action items that they will achieve. Day three reconvenes the executive team who then reviews the goals and action items from the direct reports. When I have completed this process with organizations, the goals set separately by each group of attendees usually vary by less than 2%. In all instances the action items created by the direct reports eliminated work for the executive team. The executive team was freed up to work on higher levels of the business which resulted in stronger growth and profits. Having direct reports participate in the strategic planning session creates buy-in to the goals set and drives the achievement of the goals further down into the organization.

There are six critical steps you need to take in order to prepare for your strategic planning retreat. As you complete each pre-strategy session step, you should supply the information to your executive team that will be attending the strategic planning session. Getting the information out to the attendees in advance of the strategy session will help them understand what you will be accomplishing during your strategic planning retreat.

Define your expected outcome:
You first must go through your own personal process of determining what you would like to accomplish during your planning session. This can be done by having discussions with your partners, Board of Directors, or your strategy session facilitator if you are the sole owner and CEO. You should have your facilitator involved in these meetings so they can gain insight into the goals of all the owners of your organization. I usually spend four to five hours in a private interview with my CEO clients covering two major questions. First, where do you want your company to be in five years? This question leads to a discussion about where they think the company should be as expressed in revenues and profits in the next five years. That part of the discussion includes how they expect the company to grow either through organic sales growth or with some acquisitions. The second major question I ask is where they want to be personally in five years. That discussion usually involves the CEO talking about wanting to have a high

performance management team in place that will allow the CEO to have more time away from work. Also, most CEOs and owners have a large portion, if not all, of their personal investment value tied up in their business. If the answer to the second question includes their retirement it will require that the CEO merge their personal goals with those of the business as a succession plan or plan to sell the business may need to be in place. At the end of that interview, I prepare a report to the CEO that details what I heard them say during our discussion. Having your goals in writing helps you begin the process of focusing your efforts and your organization's efforts on creating and achieving goals. This pre- strategy planning discussion helps you clarify, in your own mind, your goals for the next five years.

Pre-planning session meeting with your executive team and setting expectations for clearly defined results:
Once you have gained some clarity as to the direction you hope to take, you need to have a similar discussion with your executive team. Four to five weeks prior to the planning retreat you should share your ideas and thoughts with your executives about why you want to hold a strategy session and why the company needs a clearly defined set of strategic goals. Your strategic planning facilitator must be included in this meeting. This will begin to set the tone and parameters for discussions that will be held during your strategic planning retreat. You can tell your executive team about your general thoughts on the direction you would like to take and why you want your organization to strive for strategic alignment. This discussion might include such things as you explaining

your desire to grow the profitability of your organization, plans to make some acquisitions in the future, the intent to develop a succession plan that will allow your executive team to take over more of the management of the company, or perhaps the goal to take your company public through an Initial Public Offering in three to five years. The conversation with your executive team should not detail any specific numbers or dates but should act as a stimulus to get them thinking about the company more strategically. Generally, your key managers are working in a more tactical mode, day-to-day, and they don't get much of an opportunity to think strategically about how to move a company toward five year goals. Having this discussion with your team, usually lasting for only one to two hours, helps them understand your expectations for the upcoming strategic planning session. This discussion with your executive team will begin their process of starting to gain strategic alignment.

During this pre-planning meeting, you will discuss the purpose and expectations for the upcoming two day strategic planning retreat. It is important that you communicate to all of the planning session attendees that your two day strategic planning retreat will result in the following outcomes:

1. Three to five year strategic plan with measurable goals, such as: revenues, gross margin percentages, sales offices and clients in new geographic regions, new product lines, or growth plans through mergers or acquisitions(See chapter 4 for the 1-3-5 Method of Goal Setting™)

2. A plan for how your company will position itself in the competitive market over the upcoming three to five year period (See chapter 3). A prerequisite for this outcome is a basic analysis of your competition, industry, and how you compete with your top five competitors..

3. A set of tactical goals that will be completed by your organization in the upcoming year

Your executives must think about these critical points that you want to accomplish during your upcoming strategic planning session. Most business executives are extremely focused on their day-to-day responsibilities and activities. Getting these preliminary items to your strategic planning session attendees in advance of your planning session will assure you of their attentive participation and their understanding of what you expect the team to accomplish by the end of the strategic planning session.

Complete pre-planning session groundwork: As preparation for your strategic planning session, you and your executive team will participate in the completion of the following pre-strategy session exercises at least four weeks in advance of the planning retreat.

1. Have someone on your executive team or have your retreat facilitator research and compile data that indicates the trends that your industry will be facing over the upcoming three to five year period as detailed in chapter 3.

2. Have someone on your executive team or have your strategic planning session facilitator

complete a rating survey that compares your company's services and products with that of your top five competitors. This data will be used to complete your competitive analysis as detailed in chapter 3.

The results of the pre-strategy session work should be compiled and sent to the attendees at least one week prior to the event. This will allow them time to review the responses and be prepared to discuss the results. The data and results collected should also be consolidated into a strategic planning session binder and distributed one week in advance of the retreat. Providing this to the attendees of your planning session will give everyone a common foundation of knowledge that will be utilized in creating meaningful and achievable strategic goals.

Create an agenda: Create a well-defined agenda that clearly states what is to be accomplished each day of the planning session. Allotted times and discussion points should be identified. Expected outcomes should be defined for what needs to be accomplished by the end of each segment of the agenda. The strategy session attendees have to stay focused on the agenda and make sure that their discussions are constantly moving them toward achieving their meeting goals as guided by your facilitator. In chapter 4 you will find a detailed agenda I use for planning and organizing the strategic planning retreats.

Mandate participation: The attendees have to know they are expected to be engaged in the process of developing a strategic plan. It is very important that you do not dominate the discussion during the strategic planning session. Certain work habits are developed by the CEO and their executive team as they execute their daily work functions. In most instances, the CEO prevails in those daily discussions and decisions. The executive team usually responds with an affirmative and then goes about completing their assigned daily tasks. As part of my observation of how the team works together and who dominates the discussion in executive team meetings, I always try to attend a pre-planning meeting with a CEO and his executive team to discuss the upcoming planning retreat. In one instance, when I asked the group a question I observed that at least 50 percent of the executive team glanced over at the CEO and then waited for the CEO to answer the question. That type of CEO dominated discussion pattern will not result in a great strategic planning session. A facilitator will make sure that everyone participates with an equal voice.

When I saw this pattern in another company I asked that CEO if he would be OK with allowing the rest of the group to voice their ideas or opinions before the CEO contributed to the conversation. The CEO agreed to that discussion pattern. Once I set the tenor for discussions, within the first two hours, the group operated on an equal footing with the CEO, and the resulting dialogues were lively and inclusive. The group trusted that I would make sure that everyone at the strategy session had an equal voice and they willingly and actively participated in every discussion and decision.

I strongly recommend using an impartial, highly skilled facilitator to ensure that discussions are open, creative, and in-depth. An expert facilitator will promote participation from every attendee and make sure discussions stay focused on the strategic planning retreat goals while remaining open to all topics and ideas.

Checklist for your strategic planning session:

a. Set a date and location for strategic planning retreat.

b. Four to five Weeks ahead of Strategic Planning Session:

    i. Select a facilitator to guide your planning session.

    ii. Meet with your facilitator, Board of Directors, partners to begin to clarify your goals. Describe what you expect to accomplish at the planning retreat.

    iii. Meet with your executive team and facilitator to discuss the expected outcome of the upcoming strategic planning session.

c. Three to four weeks in advance of Strategic Planning Session

    i. Complete an industry analysis

    ii. Complete a competitive analysis

d. One week in advance of the Strategic Planning Session

    i. Distribute the planning session binder containing:

        1. The planning retreat location
        2. The agenda
        3. The industry analysis report
        4. The competitive analysis report

NOTES:

CHAPTER 3:
PRE-RETREAT WORK: INDUSTRY AND COMPETITIVE ANALYSIS

> ➢ Preparation before your strategy session
>   o Industry analysis
>   o Competitive analysis

One of the most powerful parts of your strategic planning retreat is to create a foundational understanding within your executive team about the future direction of your industry and how your company competes in its marketplace. In order to outperform your competition, you need to predict if there are going to be any changes in your industry and how you differentiate your products or services from those offered by your competition. In this chapter, I will take you through this critical part of preparing for your strategic planning session. I usually do this for my clients as part of my pre-strategy retreat preparation. I have based this chapter on the surveys and outcomes that I have generated, and I use actual results from those efforts in my examples.

If the preparation work is not being completed by your strategic planning facilitator then you have to appoint someone from your executive team to compile surveys and data from the review of your industry trend information and competitor information in advance of the planning session. That information will provide your strategic planning group with a solid base from which to start discussions about the external threats and opportunities that will challenge your organization in the near and long-term future. Completing a study of the trends in your industry will help you understand how to prepare your organization for any future industry and competitor challenges. By completing a competitive analysis you will learn how you differentiate yourself from you competitors so that you can focus your sales, marketing, and business development activities in order to maximize competitive advantage and gain market share from your competition.

It is important that this analysis be started three to four weeks in advance of your strategic planning session. You need to gather and compile data from several sources and that process can take two to three weeks. The data must be analyzed and a report completed at least one week in advance of the strategic planning retreat. This will give all of the attendees an opportunity to review the data prior to the beginning of the session.

Industry Analysis
An industry analysis is a quick investigation into the future trends of your marketplace. Many industries have at least one trade association whose members comprise your competitors and your customers. Contact your trade association, and get their projections of where they estimate your industry will be in 1, 3, and 5 years. If you operate in a single region or in several regions, get information

for global and regional industry trends. If you cannot find industry supported information, you can send out a simple survey to your employees and selected vendors. Ask for their estimations as to where they see your industry trending. Make sure that the people who receive your survey understand that they can base their opinions on their "best estimates." A survey seeking industry and competitor information need only include the following request for information:

1. What do you estimate will be the industry revenues in:

   a. Next year
   b. In two years
   c. In three years
   d. In four years
   e. In 5 years

2. Name the top five competitors in our area and estimate their annual revenues-

   a. Competitor name   Competitor Revenues $_____
   b. Competitor name   Competitor Revenues $_____
   c. Competitor name   Competitor Revenues $_____
   d. Competitor name   Competitor Revenues $_____
   e. Competitor name   Competitor Revenues $_____

During a strategy retreat with one organization, I helped the attendees create the following table based upon the survey information they compiled prior to the planning session. The organization offered their customers four different services and this table reflects their estimate of how their industry will change over the next five years:

Chart #3-1

Industry Analysis: Industry Revenue Source as a Percentage of Estimated Revenues

Service	Current Year	Next Year	3 years	5 years
Service #1	80%	70%	60%	40%
Service #2	10%	10%	10%	10%
Service #3	10%	10%	5%	0%
Service #4	0%	10%	25%	50%

By completing this Industry analysis the executive board was able to recognize the shift that was occurring in their industry. Their primary focus for the balance of the strategic planning session was on how they could best respond to these changes as they migrated through a major shift in their revenue sources.

During the pre-strategy work for another organization, a manufacturing and distribution company, I compiled the following industry data using questions similar to the survey above:

Chart #3-2

Industry Analysis: Industry Revenue Source as a Percentage of Estimated Revenues

Product	Current Year	Next Year	3 years	5 years
Product #1	50%	50%	50%	40%
Product #2	0	10%	20%	30%
Product #3	50%	40%	30%	20%

By completing the above industry analysis prior to the planning session, the executive team from this company could see the potential impact of the changes in their sales and manufacturing operations over the next 5 years. The analysis revealed to them that they needed to create strategic plans for handling those changes.

Completing an industry analysis will provide you with insight on whether or not there are any major changes facing your industry. If there are major shifts in your industry over the next three to five years, your strategic planning retreat will have to address how your organization will respond to those changes.

The information that you compile for your industry will also be utilized while you are completing the goal setting portion of your strategy session which I discuss in detail in chapter 5.

Competitive Analysis

Completing a competitive analysis will help you and your executive team better understand how you compete in your marketplace. In a competitive analysis you will identify the advantage that you hold over your competitors. Your competitive advantage is measured by how much you differentiate your products or services from those of your competitors. You should complete your competitive analysis three to four weeks prior to your strategic planning retreat so that your attendees have one week in advance to review the compiled data.

Competitive Factors

The first step in a competitive analysis is to identify the competitive factors of your industry. Competitive factors influence a customer's buying decision. Here are some examples of common competitive factors:

1. Price
2. Quality of products or services
3. Customer Service
4. Financial Stability
5. Location

Identify what you think are the competitive factors for your company. Get feedback from your customers, vendors, and employees. Limit your competitive factors to the top five for your company and your industry.

Competitive Factor Weighting

Once you have identified your competitive factors, you need to estimate how much influence each of the factors has on your customer's buying decision. In the following examples, I based my sample survey on an industry where the customers identified and rated the competitive factors that influenced their buying decisions as follows:

Price	40%
Quality	35%
Customer Service (product knowledge)	15%
Financial Stability	5%
Location	5%

Identify your competitive factors and then get feedback from customers, vendors, and employees.

Competitors

The next step is to identify your top five competitors. Your top competitors compete with you to sell similar products or services to the same customer base, region, etc. that you service.

Collect and compile the data

After you have defined your competitive factors and named your competitors, put them into a survey that you will send to employees, selected customers, and selected vendors. This part of your survey asks for their rating of how your company competes on the various factors as compared to your competitors. Have at least ten to fifteen people, try to get as many responses as you can, fill out the table using a rating system of 1-10 with 1=Not competitive to 10=Extremely Competitive. The following is an example of a completed competitive analysis data table:

Chart #3-3

Competitor Ratings (10=most competitive 1=least competitive)

Competitor	Price	Quality	Customer Service	Financial Stability	Location
Your Company	8	10	10	8	7
Competitor #1	10	6	6	7	7
Competitor #2	9	6	5	5	7
Competitor #3	9	5	5	5	7
Competitor #4	7	7	8	6	7
Competitor #5	7	7	7	5	7

Have those that fill out the table above also complete an estimation of how much the competitive factors influence their buying decision.

Chart #3-4

Competitive Factor Ratings

Competitive Factor	% of importance in buying decision
Price	40%
Quality	35%
Customer Service	15%
Financial Stability	5%
Location	5%
Total (Must equal 100%)	100%

Collect all of the surveys and average out the results from all of the data.

Competitive Analysis
Raw data
You will complete two types of analysis of the collected data -unadjusted data analysis and adjusted/weighted data analysis. The unadjusted data analysis takes the data collected and averages the results of the raw data from all of the surveys. Based upon the tables above the, following is an example of a graph of the unadjusted data from a competitive analysis survey:

Chart #3-5

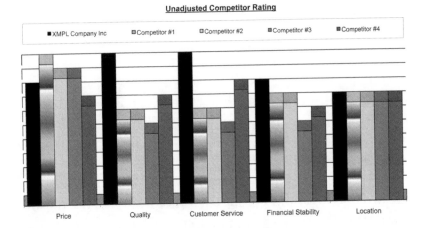

Unadjusted Competitor Rating

| ■XMPL Company Inc | ▣Competitor #1 | ▢Competitor #2 | ▨Competitor #3 | ▥Competitor #4 |

Price Quality Customer Service Financial Stability Location

Competitive analysis of the raw data

The analysis of this unadjusted data in Chart #3-5shows the XMPL Company (black) is the highest rated in quality and customer service. In all of the other competitive factors XMPL Company is at least on an "at par" level or just a little below all of its competitors. XMPL Company clearly differentiates itself from its competitors in quality and customer service. These are its competitive advantages. You can see from the data that competitor #1is XMPL Company's main price competitor, but they have a low score in quality and customer service. In order to exploit the differentiation against Competitor #1 XMPL Company should emphasize its quality of product and exemplary customer service.

Complete your company's competitive analysis to determine your differentiation. With that knowledge, you can focus your sales, marketing, and business development programs to emphasize your strengths. If you have a product that differentiates you from your competitors, make sure your product promotion and product development programs perpetuate that front running market position. If you have no clear differentiation, then you and your executive team must determine how you want to differentiate your products or services and then develop and execute your programs to drive you to the dominant position for that competitive factor.

Adjusted/Weighted Data

The next step in a competitive analysis is to apply the average weighting of the competitive factors by adjusting the raw data with the weighting factor in order to see how you differentiate your products or services based upon their influence on a customer's buying decision. If you focus a huge amount of effort on a competitive factor that is unimportant to the buying decision, you are wasting your time and money.

Using the weighting factors (how much the buying decision is based upon a competitive factor) the following is an example of the above raw data that has been adjusted by the weighting of each competitive factor:

Chart #3-6

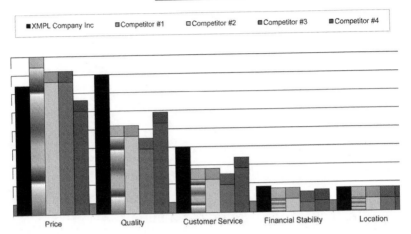

Competitive analysis of the weighted data

The chart above shows that the primary influence on the buying decision is price with quality being the second most important competitive factor. Based upon the survey results XMPL Company's (black) customers rate it a little below par as compared to its three major competitors when it comes to pricing. If XMPL Company's customers base their decision solely on price, they will buy from its competitors. If XMPL Company's customers are concerned about quality and customer service, they will buy from XMPL Company more than they will buy from its competitors. XMPL Company's customers know that they will pay a little bit more, but they also understand that XMPL Company's far superior quality and service are worth the extra cost. XMPL Company's tactics for gaining market share from its competitors must focus on the lack of quality of the competitors' products and the added value the customer receives by purchasing the higher quality products of XMPL Company.

One company I worked with completed their competitive analysis only to find that both the organization and their eight competitors were all doing a mediocre job of delivering the five competitive factors from their industry. Neither the company nor its competitors had a clear competitive advantage. During the strategic planning session, the executive team decided to focus on one of the competitive factors to make it their clear competitive advantage. The balance of the strategic planning session involved identifying what they needed to do and who would get it done, to ensure they held a clear competitive advantage by the end of the year.

Study the results of your industry and competitive analysis with your executive team during your strategy session in order to identify and understand your industry trends and company's differentiators. Your discussions during your planning session should focus on your company's efforts to dominate your competition with your differentiation. You have to establish how you will emphasize your differentiation in all of your sales, business development, product development, and marketing activities in order to gain market share. After your planning retreat you should continuously, at least two times per year, update the industry and competitive analysis data. This will constantly keep you alert to what your competition is doing and where your industry is headed.

Checklist for industry and competitive analysis:

1. Identify trends in your industry (four to five weeks in advance of your strategic planning session)

   a. Contact trade associations
   b. Survey to customers

2. Competitive Analysis (four to five weeks in advance of your strategic planning session)

   a. Rate your own products and services
   b. Rate your competitor's products and services
   c. Compile data

3. Organize industry and competitive analyses into your retreat binder and distribute it to your strategic planning session attendees (one week in advance of your strategic planning session

4. Review and update data continuously

NOTES:

CHAPTER 4:
PRE RETREAT WORK:
STRATEGIC PLANNING
SESSION AGENDA

Agenda for strategic planning session

1. Day One

    i. Review and discuss industry analysis data
    ii. Review and discuss competitive analysis data
    iii. create strategic goals for the organization
        1. Utilize 1-3-5 Method of Goal Setting™ (Chapter 5)

    iv. Begin to create twelve month tactical objectives

2. Day Two

    i. Complete twelve month tactical objectives
        1. Identify executive team ownership of objectives
    ii. Convert twelve month tactical objectives into deliverables (Chapter 8)
    iii. Review strategic goals
    iv. Create communication plan (Chapter 9)
    v. Create meeting schedule for executive team strategic plan reviews

In the first three chapters we have covered the work that you will complete in preparation for your strategic planning retreat. In the next four chapters we will go through what you will accomplish during your actual strategic planning session. The outline above is the agenda summary that I utilize when I lead teams through a strategic planning session. In addition to the summarized agenda I also create a detailed agenda in which I describe what will be accomplished during each segment of the upcoming planning retreat. I send the description of the agenda segments out to the attendees of the strategic planning retreat at least one week in advance of the planning session so that they can have a preview of what will occur at the session. This chapter provides you with an agenda blueprint you can use to plan your own upcoming strategic planning retreat.

Detailed Agenda-Strategic Planning Session
Day one: The purpose of the strategic planning session is to start the process of transforming your company into a strategically aligned organization that is able to successfully achieve its strategic goals.

During day one of the strategic planning retreat, you and your executive team will gain a deeper understanding of your industry and the competitors of your company Building upon that foundation of knowledge, you and your team will then begin to create your strategic goals. Once you have created your strategic goals you will begin to identify specific actions that must be taken in the upcoming twelve months in order to move your organization toward achieving your long-term strategic goals.

Agenda Item #1: Review Expected Outcome of Planning Session

During the first few minutes of your strategic planning retreat, it is important to have a quick review of your expectations for the outcome of your strategy session. This should be a review of the topics you discussed with your executives during your pre-strategy session preparation as detailed in chapter 2.

You should also make sure that everyone understands that you want an open dialogue on all topics and your expectation is that everyone must participate in the discussions.

Agenda Item #2: Review and discuss industry analysis data

In chapter 3, you learned how to complete an industry analysis to understand the trends and changes that are occurring in your industry. This information was collected, compiled and then distributed to all of the attendees prior to the strategic planning retreat. In my experience, very few of the attendees will review the data prior to the planning session. Many of them do not understand the significance of the industry trend analysis, so it is important to have a detailed discussion about the data. Take the time at this point in your strategy session to review the industry and competitive analysis data and have a discussion about how this knowledge should be used by your organization during your goal setting session.

I led an executive board through the review of their industry data. Many on the team did not review the data prior to the strategy session and did not understand its importance.

As I led them through the industry review and discussion, the team recognized that one of their principal revenue generators was going to lose 50 percent of its revenues in the upcoming five years as their customers shifted to new technology. Their review of the industry data had a huge impact on their setting realistic strategic goals for the next five years and added to the discussion about how their organization would respond to this industry shift.

Agenda Item #3: Review and discuss competitive analysis data

In chapter 3, you also learned how to complete a competitive analysis to understand how you compete in your marketplace, who your competitors are, and what differentiates your company from all of your competitors. This information was collected, compiled, and then distributed to all of the attendees prior to the strategic planning retreat. Just like the industry analysis data, very few of the attendees will review the competitive analysis data prior to the planning session and many of them do not understand its importance. You will need to review all of the data and discuss your competitive advantage and how you should exploit that differentiation.

Agenda Item #4: Create strategic goals

The next part of your session agenda is where you will create your strategic goals and then test their reality. With the foundation of knowledge that you possess after a thorough discussion of the industry and competitive analysis data, you can begin filling in the basic information using the 1-3-5 Method of Goal Setting™ forms which are discussed in complete detail in chapter 5. During this section of the planning retreat you will continually discuss and test the reality of all of the goals that you are creating. I have found that this is always a highly interactive discussion. You and your executive team must go through a detailed review of all of the challenges and potential roadblocks that you will face as you move toward achieving your strategic goals.

Strategic goals are large targets that contain few details. They are a view of your company in five years from the fifty thousand foot level. They are usually high level targets like revenues, new branches in target cities, new revenue sources, and profit levels. They may also include acquisitions, mergers, and even IPO plans if you are not a publicly traded company. Creating the details for each of these strategic goals will be added to your plan when you begin creating tactical objectives for the upcoming twelve month period.

Agenda Item #5: Creating twelve month tactical objectives

Once you have agreed upon your strategic goals, you begin the process of identifying what you have to do in order to achieve those strategic goals. Your discussions now begin to get more detailed. If the strategic goals are view from the fifty thousand foot level, then the twelve month tactical objectives are a view from the ten thousand foot level. This is a brainstorming session where you take each strategic goal and identify all of the things that you must begin over the next twelve months in order to start actualizing your five year strategic goals. As an example, if a strategic goal is to increase your number of branch offices, your tactical objective might be to identify your three top desired locations. As another example, if your strategic goal is to increase your gross margin to a set percentage of sales, you might set a tactical goal of achieving an incremental increase within the next twelve months. Chapters 5-8 will provide you with greater detail on how to identify and define tactical objectives.

It is best to limit your tactical objectives to no more than five items that will be completed in the upcoming twelve months. In my experience of leading companies through this process, I have found that having more than five tactical objectives tends to scatter the focus of an organization. Later on in the planning session these objectives will be broken down into tasks and assigned to executive team members with measurable expectations and timelines during the planning session. The attendees must understand that it's the responsibility of the executive team to drive the achievement of your company's goals down to the desktop of every employee starting immediately after the conclusion of the strategic planning retreat. (See chapter 8 for converting these goals into deliverables.)

DAY TWO:

Agenda Item #6: Converting twelve month tactical objectives into deliverables

With your twelve month tactical objectives identified, you will now work on who has the responsibility of delivering the goals. Each member of the executive team will be held accountable for the achievement of specified tactical objectives. During this section of the strategic planning retreat, the entire executive team will participate in identifying the individual action items that will need to be completed in order to achieve the goals of the twelve month tactical objectives. If the twelve month tactical objectives were a ten thousand foot view, this part of the process brings the detail down to the one thousand foot level. The final details, at sea level, will come during the review and discussions with all of the rest of your employees when you return to your offices after your strategic planning retreat. As an example, if your tactical objective was to identify three desired cities for new branches, one of the deliverables might be to complete a market analysis of ten cities in order to determine which ones fulfill your branch operation requirements. That's the type of detail that is created in this section of the strategic planning session. You will find this subject covered in greater detail in chapters 7 and 8.

Agenda Item #7: Reviewing your strategic goals

After you have divided your twelve month tactical objectives into individual action items, it is time to revisit your strategic goals. This is another spot in your planning session where you will look at all of the details and ask yourselves if there is any identifiable reason your company will be unable to achieve your goals. As an example, let's say one of your strategic goals is to make an acquisition of another business to expand your marketplace. As you and your executive team developed your twelve month goals you determined that it was going to require 50 percent of the time of your executive team to be involved in that acquisition. As your discussions delved deeper into the details of an acquisition you found that your ongoing business could not survive with the executive team un-involved in the day-to-day business. At that point, you would have to discuss whether or not to alter your strategic goal to make an acquisition, if you should hire an outside acquisition advisor, or if you should extend the timing of the acquisition so that you can sustain your business while making the acquisition. A review of the details behind executing all action items may reveal some aspects of a strategic goal that had not been considered. Having your executive team involved in the creation of the detailed action items will help you and your team discover any roadblocks and determine if they can be avoided or if the strategic goals have to be set at a different level. By continuously revisiting your strategic goals you will put them to a reality test and confirm whether or not they are achievable.

Agenda Item #8: Create communication plan

During this section of your planning session you will work on your schedule for reviewing and communicating the strategic goals to 100 percent of your employees. Your entire company is aware of the fact that you and your executive team have been away from the office creating a strategic plan. Upon returning to your offices, you need to let every employee know the outcome of your planning session. At this point in the planning retreat you will all agree on the approach and message that is to be delivered to each team so that there is a clear and consistent message being communicated in a timely manner. You may also decide that you want to hold a brief all-company meeting where you personally deliver the goals and objectives to 100 percent of your employees. This is the beginning of exposed accountability for the executive team. Once the whole company knows about the goals and the action plan for the upcoming twelve months, your executive team will be fully responsible for the achievement of those goals. At this point, you should also set dates and times when each executive member will meet with their respective teams. Converting the goals into date-specific deliverables will help your executives delegate pieces of that responsibility out to 100 percent of your employees. You will find this subject covered in greater detail in chapters 7, 8, and 9.

Agenda Item #9: Create meeting schedule for executive team strategic plan reviews

The final item to be covered by you and your executive team before leaving the strategic planning session is to set the dates and times for your strategic plan reviews. The first review will occur within two weeks after the end of the planning session. Subsequent reviews should be scheduled at least once every ninety days. These meetings require participation by all the attendees of your strategic planning retreat, and getting these dates in your executive team members' calendars is critical. Having set review dates emphasizes the principle of exposed accountability. Your executives will know that there will be plan reviews and updates throughout the year and that they will have to report their progress and the achievements of their team on the dates that you set up during this final step in your strategic planning process. Earlier in chapter 1, I stated that most strategic plans begin to fail within two weeks. They begin to fail because the executive team did not set dates and times where they will report on their progress, or lack of it, to the rest of the executive team. Your team needs to hold each other accountable. Quarterly strategic plan reviews will help make that happen.

Flip Charts as a Tool

I utilize Post It Note flip charts (25" x 30"), set up on an easel to record all aspects of the session: the discussion points, any goal setting or brainstorming ideas and the deliverable action items. The use of flip charts helps do two important things: 1) it establishes a record of the key points in a discussion and 2) it provides visibility into the work that has been accomplished during the planning retreat. I use the Post It brand because it is self-adhesive and by the end of a two-day strategic planning session, I may completely envelop walls and windows with flip charts covered with information. I take photos of all of the flip chart pages and use them to create my strategic planning retreat report, as well as tracking documents that contain deliverables and action items (Chapter 8 and 9). I utilize standard marking pens that have a large enough tip to provide for visibility. I reserve the red colored marking pen for action items, exclusively. At the end of each day the red action items stand out on the flip charts and provide the participants with a clear view of the deliverables that have been created during the strategic planning session.

One of my clients took all of the flip chart pages from the planning retreat back to their own conference room and hung them on the walls so that everyone in the organization could see the work that had been accomplished during the two-day planning session. For the next several months, whenever they had team meetings to work on the achievement of their strategic planning goals, they held those meetings in their conference room with all of the flip chart pages still on the walls.

Flip charts are an easy way to provide visibility into how goals were established and how deliverable action items were created. Several of my clients have told me that they now have a blank flip chart set up for every meeting so that they are ready to capture brainstorming ideas and record action items that are created during a meeting.

NOTES:

CHAPTER 5:
1-3-5 METHOD FOR GOAL SETTING™

> ➤ Establishing goals for 1, 3 and 5 years
> ➤ Putting goals to a reality test
>   o Industry trends
>   o Setting your company goals for revenues
>   ▪ Company historical performance
>   o Competitor activity
>   o Setting other company performance goals
>   ▪ Company historical performance

Goal setting is one of the most important outcomes of a strategic planning session. It has been estimated that only 3% of organizations have established a three year or five year goal. Having 1, 3 and 5-year goals that are clearly stated, will give you a competitive advantage. It is further estimated that less than 1% of organizations communicate their goals to 100% of their employees. Putting your goals to a reality test is a critical step in assuring that your goals are achievable. Over the years, I have developed a method of goal setting that I have trademarked as the 1-3-5 Method for Goal Setting™. Most organizations approach their analysis of industry data, competitive data and goal setting as separate and distinct functions.

My 1-3-5 Method of Goal Setting™ process merges the review and utilization of your industry analysis data, competitive analysis data, and your internal data into a single document. As you proceed through your planning session you will continually refer back to this document as you validate whether or not your goals are realistic and achievable

During your goal setting you will create the 1-3-5 Method for Goal Setting™ data table like the one in chart #5-1. As you complete the 1-3-5 Method for Goal Setting™, you will be checking the authenticity and achievability of each goal. It is important to remember that the goals you establish will be the foundation of deliverables for 100 percent of your employees for the next twelve months. Everyone will be held accountable for the delivery of their individual action items. It is critical that the goals created during the strategic planning session are based on reliable assumptions. This requires in-depth discussions during the goal setting section of the strategic planning retreat.

It is important to understand that if goals are set so high that they exceed any reasonable expectation to meet them they will serve as a discouragement to your teams. If your organization knows that the goals are unrealistic and unattainable, they will not work to achieve them. I worked with one company where the CEO set the revenue goals every year. He created the goals without any input from his team and he based the goals on a generalized percentage growth over the prior year. When the goals came down to the sales team you could hear complaints throughout the company. In order to keep this from becoming a disincentive to the sales teams, I suggested to the CEO that he allow each divisional sales team to provide him with their market-based goals. The resulting goals that came out of that process were in some instances higher than what the CEO had initially budgeted but they were realistic and they were supported by validated market data. In addition, the CEO and the executive team understood the value in having the new goals created by the sales team. They understood that the sales team had researched and validated their goals. In doing so the sales team had assumed total responsibility for setting and achieving those goals.

The goals you set using the 1-3-5 Method of Goal Setting™ will be based on real information. You will test that they are achievable and that they will push your organization to operate at its absolute best in order to achieve them. In all of the strategic planning retreats that I have facilitated a specified level of revenues is always the first goal in their five year plan. Since it is always the number one strategic goal I will use revenues to demonstrate the 1-3-5 Method of Goal Setting™.

Industry trends and forecasting your company's revenue
In chapter 3, I talked about forecasting where your Industry was heading in one year, three years, and five years. With that data in hand you can begin your goal setting at your strategic planning session. As you forecast your company's revenue goals for the same period of time you will compare your forecasts with that of your industry over the next 1, 3, and 5 years.

Begin your goal setting by completing a forecast of your company's revenues. Using your current year revenues as the starting point, forecast where your revenues will be in one year, three years and five years. Most companies simplify this projection by adding a percentage of growth to their current year's revenues. That's the simplest way to start the process. As you step through the 1-3-5 Method for Goal Setting™ you will test the validity of your initial goals by comparing your projections with the industry forecasts for the same period. Are you maintaining your market share, growing your market share, or losing market share? As you review your strategic goals, validate the reality of your goals. As an example, if your projected growth exceeds the projected growth of your industry you need to discuss why you think you will be able to exceed industry trends. (See chart #5-1)

In order to further validate your goals, you must divide your revenues into product or service lines that your company offers and complete the same 1-3-5 Method for Goal Setting™ for each of those product or service lines. Discuss how each line will provide growth or see declines in revenues. Add up all of the components of your revenues and validate that they equal the sum of your 1-3-5 year goals for the company. Make sure that you discuss what will cause your revenues to grow or decline so that everyone understands the impact of industry or competitive factors on your revenues. Discuss how each product or service line will grow and how your organization will respond to support and drive those changes in revenues. (See chart #5-1)

As a further reality test of your market place, estimate the current year revenues for your competitors. This entails listing your top four to five competitors and their revenue estimates. It is important to understand that this does not have to be an exact revenue estimate. Completing this review will give you a better understanding as to where you rank in your market place. Understanding your competitors' positions in the market place will also help you evaluate the reality of your goals. As an example, if you feel that your competitive advantage allows you to outperform one or two of your key competitors; will it allow you to take market share away from them in the future? Do your strategic goals account for that increase in market share? Using the 1-3-5 Method for Goal Setting™ constantly provides you with a way to confirm the reality and achievability of your goals.

Here is an example of how your compilation of data should look after you have completed the 1-3-5 Method for Goal Setting™ during your strategic planning session:

Chart #5-1

1-3-5 Method of Goal Setting Data

Product/Service Source of Revenue	Current Year	1 year	3 year	5 year
Industry Total	$500,000,000	$550,000,000	$600,000,000	$720,000,000
Company Total	$40,000,000	$42,000,000	$46,000,000	$54,000,000
Company's Market Share	8%	7.6%	7.7%	7.5%
Competitor #1 Share of Market	$60,000,000			
Competitor #2 Share of Market	$100,000,000			
Competitor #3 Share of Market	$75,000,000			
Competitor #4 Share of Market	$95,000,000			
All other competitors	$130,000,000			

Product/Service Source of Revenue	Current Year	1 year	3 year	5 year
Company Components of Total Revenue	$40,000,000	$42,000,000	$46,000,000	$54,000,000
Product/Service Line #1	$25,000,000	$22,000,000	$20,000,000	$20,000,000
Product/Service Line #2	$5,000,000	$8,000,000	$12,000,000	$22,000,000
Product/Service Line #3	$7,000,000	$8,000,000	$8,000,000	$8,000,000
Product/Service Line #4	$3,000,000	$4,000,000	$4,000,000	$4,000,000

Once you have completed the 1-3-5 Method for Goal Setting™ for your revenues you can continue to use the same method to set strategic goals for other segments of your operations represented in the chart #5-2:

Chart #5-2

Examples of Other 1-3-5 Strategic Goals

Strategic Goal	Current Year	1 Year	3 Year	5 Year
Gross Margin % of revenues	44%	45%	46%	48%
G&A Expenses % of revenues	18%	18%	17.5%	17.%
Inventory Turns	5.5	6.0	7.0	8.5
Profits	5%	6%	7.5%	10%

Using the 1-3-5 Method for Goal Setting™ during your strategic planning session will provide you and your executive team with reality tested goals that are attainable and measurable. An important aspect of goal setting is that each goal must be defined in terms of a benchmark measurement. As an example, one company I worked with wanted to be known as one of the best places to work in its region. One of their measurements of that goal was their turnover rate of employees. Their industry average turnover rate was 22 percent, and they set their goal to be 15 percent or less. I have found that almost every goal can be measured in some form or another. If a goal cannot be definitively measured, then it cannot be identified as a goal. Without a form of measurement, you cannot measure progress toward the goal. If you cannot measure a goal then you will be unable ascertain when you have reached the goal. During the compilation of the data, you and your team will have had discussions about your industry, your competitors, whether or not you can take market share from your competitors, what products or service lines will be growing or contracting, and why your company can achieve its goals. During a typical strategic planning session the 1-3-5 Method for Goal Setting™ is completed within the first two to four hours of day one. The remainder of the strategic planning retreat is then dedicated to the details of how you will achieve your goals and what actions are necessary to reach those goals.

Checklist for goal setting:
- Compile the 1-3-5 Method for Goal Setting™ during the first segment of your planning session

  o Forecast your market place
  o Predict your competitive standing in your market place

- Test the reality of your goals
- Discuss strategies on how to attain your goals

NOTES:

CHAPTER 6:
CREATIVE BRAINSTORMING

Brainstorming is an effective tool for collecting the creative ideas of your group or organization in order to solve a problem or create a strategic goal. The purpose of a brainstorming session is to create an opportunity for everyone to share their ideas about how to solve a problem or reach a goal. The worst idea is the one that never gets expressed. Brainstorming is used most effectively when you create a tone that promotes spontaneity. A great brainstorming session should produce some ideas that you may otherwise never have explored as an organization.

As I mentioned in Chapter 1, a key benefit derived from a spontaneous brainstorming session is the discovery of self-limiting beliefs. Exposing a self-limiting belief during a brainstorming session allows an executive team to identify the areas in which they can lead their company to greater levels of success.

Leading a team through the process
I begin a brainstorming session with a prompt such as, "How can you grow your revenues by 15% next year?" or "What are the steps you would take to solve a problem?" I then turn my back to the room and start writing down all

of the ideas. Once the room goes quiet for 30-60 seconds I turn around and make sure that they have exhausted all trains of thought. I have led brainstorming sessions where I have filled 4-5 pages of flip charts with ideas in response to only one question.

Using a flip chart to record the brainstorming ideas allows everyone to see all of the responses and will provide you with a platform for completing the brainstorming process that includes three steps:

1. Collecting spontaneous ideas
2. Consolidating the ideas into major topics
3. Prioritizing those major topics into steps you will take to solve your problem or reach your goal.

Step one: With a flip chart on an easel and marking pen in hand, clearly state the problem to address or the goal to be identified. I led a Washington company through a planning session where they decided one of the main goals for the year was to improve their customer service department. Their practice up to that point had been to have the sales team handle customer service. However, there were issues with follow up and consistent complaints. In addition, each member of the sales team was spending at least 10-15 hours per week handling customer service work. The executive team clearly stated that the two main goals to be achieved with a new customer service department were:

1. All customer inquiries would be handled within 1-2 hours of receiving the inquiry

Every inquiry would be responded to by customer service before the end of every business day.

2. Each member of the sales team would gain 10-15 hours per week for growing revenues and strengthening customer relationships (they had 10 full time sales people=100+ hours per week of selling).

I led the executive team through a brainstorming session which began with the question "What do you think a world-class customer service department should look like at your company?" I then wrote down all of their spontaneous responses as follows:

Quick response to customers

Dedicated staff to customer service

Stronger relationships with customers

Communication with customers

After sale service and support to customers

Handling any warranty issues

Handle customer questions

Standardized procedures

Standardized forms and documents

Follow up with factory orders for on time delivery

Coordination of product delivery

Scheduling and coordinating customer training on products

Manage all warranty claims by customers

Coordinate with project teams and project managers

Step two: The group then consolidated their responses into three main topics and grouped their brainstorming responses under each of those major topics.

Dedicated full time customer service team

Dedicated staff to customer service

Communication with customers and sales team

Communication with customers

After sale service and support to customers

Handling any warranty issues

Handle customer questions

Quick response to customers

Stronger relationships with customers

Standardized processes, procedures and forms

Standardized procedures

Standardized forms and documents

Follow up with factory orders for on time delivery

Coordination of product delivery

Scheduling and coordinating customer training on products

Manage all warranty claims by customers

Coordinate with project teams and project managers

Step three: The executive team prioritized the major topics in order to manage the process of creating a world-class customer service department. The prioritized list then became the focus for creating action items and timetables for the delivery of each of the major topics. The prioritized list was as follows:

1. Dedicated full time customer service department
2. Standardized processes, procedures and forms
3. Communication with customers and sales team

I use brainstorming in all of my strategic planning sessions with a variety of subjects, including:

How do we grow our sales with current customers?

What should we do to improve our website?

How can we improve employee morale?

What can we do to improve project management?

How can we improve quality of our manufactured products?

How would you identify the perfect customer for our services?

Where should we open a branch operation?

Once you have completed the three steps of your brainstorming session: 1) collecting ideas, 2) consolidating ideas into major topics and 3) prioritizing, you will utilize mind mapping as a tool to convert each of the major topics into deliverable action items as detailed in the next chapter.

Brainstorming is all about collecting ideas in a spontaneous and creative way that gets everyone involved. You never know who will come up with a really great idea. Game changing ideas have come from many of my strategic planning sessions when brainstorming was used as the start of the process. Keep it free-flowing and fun. You will be amazed with the ideas and practical solutions that you and your team develop using creative brainstorming.

NOTES:

CHAPTER 7:
MIND MAPPING TOOL

Mind mapping takes the ideas from your brainstorming session and converts them into deliverable action items that delegate activities to individuals or teams. When those deliverable action items are completed, your organization will achieve its goals or resolve its issues. Mind mapping will also provide you and your team with visibility into how each deliverable action item is linked to the achievement of a goal and how 100% of your employees can contribute to the successful delivery of your strategic plan goals.

The goal of the Washington based company from the previous brainstorming chapter was to create a world-class customer service department. After the three steps were completed in the brainstorming session, I took the executive team through a mind mapping exercise that further identified the next steps they would need to take in order to create deliverable action items.

Using that goal (world-class customer service) as the top of the mind map (see diagram 7-1) and the three major topics (staff, processes and communication) from the brainstorming session, the diagram below identifies the various segments of the goal. Under the dedicated staff section, the executive team determined that they needed to create a deliverable that would result in the interviewing of the current staff to see who wanted to be part the customer service group. That deliverable became an action item. The process was repeated for the recruiting of additional customer service employees with the creation of another deliverable action item. Once the dedicated staff section was planned, the discussion and mind mapping process shifted to each of the other two sections 1) Processes and procedures and 2) communications. Those two main topics were segmented into smaller steps and deliverable action items were created, as depicted in diagram 7-1. Diagram 7-1 is an example of a mind map diagram. During the strategic planning retreat I drew this up on a flip chart in front of the entire executive team. In a normal planning session there may be a mind map for every major goal that has been segmented into deliverable action items.

Example: Mind mapping #7-1

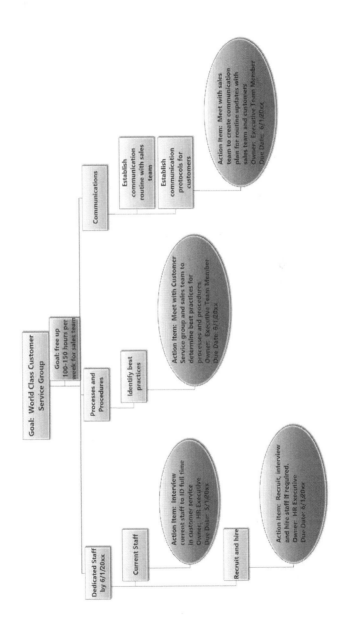

NOTES:

CHAPTER 8:
CONVERTING GOALS
INTO DELIVERABLES

> ➤ Convert long term strategic goals into current year objectives
> ➤ Identify which member of your executive team will be accountable for achieving specific goals
>   o Break each current year goal into actionable items
> ➤ Review and reality test all of your 1-3-5 Method for Goal Setting™ goals

The first segments of your strategic planning retreat have been dedicated to creating strategic goals that are real and attainable. As I stated before, this should be completed within the first two to four hours of day one of your strategy planning session. By now, you have set the tone of your session and provided a foundation for you and your executive team to build plans on how to succeed in the delivery of all of your strategic goals. During the remainder of your planning session, you and your executive team will focus on the steps you will take in order to achieve your strategic goals.

The next segment of your strategic planning retreat involves detailing your strategic goals into twelve month goals resulting in smaller measurable tasks that will be completed by you, your executives, and their teams. These twelve month goals are much more tactical goals since their objectives will be reached during your upcoming operating year. By breaking your strategic goals into tactical goals and then breaking your tactical goals into deliverables, you and your executive team are beginning to drive the achievement of your strategic goals down through your entire organization. You should limit your tactical objectives to no more than five major goals that will be completed in the upcoming twelve months. In my experience, most organizations get too scattered if they try to complete more than five key goals in a twelve month period.

Your planning facilitator will lead you through a brainstorming session that will help you break your twelve month goals into more detailed action items that usually results in a list of fifteen to twenty deliverables per strategic goal you need to accomplish. Once you have your brainstorming list completed for a single twelve month goal, you will have to prioritize and consolidate your objectives. In most instances several of your deliverables can be consolidated into a single broadly defined goal. The process of prioritizing and consolidating tactical objectives should result in paring your brainstorming list down to five to eight priority items. In the end, the top five priority items become the twelve month tactical objectives that you will then break down into more detailed deliverables including measurable goals and timelines. If you have more than five tactical objectives the remaining items are held at the sidelines and can be added to the twelve month tactical objectives list after one of the top five has been successfully completed.

In chapter 5, 1-3-5 Method of Goal Setting™, the examples I used were based upon the strategic goals of increasing revenues, improving gross margins, decreasing general and administrative expenses, and increasing inventory turns. We'll continue to expand on those examples to demonstrate converting strategic goals into deliverable action items. Chart #8-1 reflects where we left our discussion and examples after setting 1-3-5 goals for Example Company.

The following are examples of how your brainstorming session can lead you to establish accountability by breaking the larger goals into smaller elements to be completed by the teams that report to your executive team members.

In the example from chart #8-1 the one year goal of increasing revenues from $40M to $42M was further detailed by what product or service lines would provide the changes in revenues. During this phase of the strategic planning retreat, you and your executive team will discuss how you plan to meet the revenue goals for each product/service line. You will also identify who on the executive team will be held accountable for the achievement of the goals. At the same time, you will determine if the identified executive member will have someone that will partner with them to help achieve the goal and its identified deliverables.

Chart #8-1

Five Strategic Goals for Example Company (from chapter 5)

Strategic Goal	Current Year	1 Year	3 Year	5 Year
Gross Revenues	$40,000,000	$4,200,000	$46,000,000	$54,000,000
Product or Service Line #1	$25,000,000	$22,000,000	$20,000,000	$20,000,000
Product or Service Line #2	$5,000,000	$8,000,000	$12,000,000	$22,000,000
Product or Service Line #3	$7,000,000	$8,000,000	$8,000,000	$8,000,000
Product or Service Line #4	$3,000,000	$4,000,000	$4,000,000	$4,000,000
Gross Margin % of revenues	44%	45%	46%	48%
G&A Expenses % of revenues	18%	18%	17.5%	17.%
Inventory Turns	5.5	6.0	7.0	8.5
Profits	5%	6%	7.5%	10%

Beginning with the increase in revenues in year one you identify the goals, the responsible executive, and if there is anyone else on the executive team who will partner with them to deliver the goals. Not every twelve month goal will require that someone have an identified partner. It is not unusual for a goal's achievement to be the responsibility of a single executive team member. Here's an example of how you should break out the details of a twelve month tactical objective:

Goal: Increase revenues by $2.0M in year 1 (from chart #8-1)
    Product #1 decrease in revenues $2.0M

    Product #2 increase in revenues $3.0M

    Product #3 Increase in revenues $1.0M

    Product #4 Increase in revenues $1.0M

Responsible executive: Director of Sales
Partner: Director of Marketing
As you discuss the goal and its detailed components like revenue changes by product line, you and your team will identify more detailed action items that need to be completed for each goal. Those detailed action items become measureable deliverables with goals, due dates, and designated individual(s) who is responsible for the completion of a deliverable. You need to chart these detailed action items in a table like chart #8-2 while you are having these discussions during your strategic planning session.

These detailed discussions should involve the entire executive team and should continually address the reality of the goals you have set and how they are going to be achieved. The final document created will serve as your common point of reference and will be utilized by the executive team for tracking progress toward the achievement of your year one goals. The individual who is accountable for the delivery of the goal will utilize the input from the entire executive team for gathering ideas and suggestions for ways to achieve the established goals. This document will also become the tracking document for deliverables for whoever is listed as being responsible in the accountability column (See chart #8-2). During this process, you will identify detailed action items to be completed so that the twelve month tactical objective can be achieved.

In chart #8-2 the twelve month tactical goal is for the sales team to increase revenues by $2.0M. Chart #8-2 depicts the actual work product from one of my facilitated strategic planning retreats. The executive team discussed and identified specific activities that needed to be completed in order for the sales team to deliver the twelve month revenue goals. Each action item identifies who will be responsible for completing the task, when it is due, and the measurement that indicates when the goal it will be reached.

There can be no ambiguity as to the due date and the measurement of the action item. The due date should be detailed down to the hour of the day that the task is completed. I have heard conversations within teams debating whether or not due dates were met because the time of day was too vague. In a discussion at a client's office the

due date was stated as "March 15 end of business day."
The conversation went something like this:

> "I wasn't late. I completed the task at 11:00 p.m. so
> I met my due date."

> "The due date is the end of the business day."

> "Well, the end of my business day is midnight!"

> "But I needed it by 5:00 p.m. so that I could plan my
> actions for the next morning meeting."

These types of nit-picking issues can impair your ability
to keep your team communicating and focused on the
achievement of your goals. They are distracting and can
be harmful to your goal of achieving strategic alignment.
You can avoid such conflicts by being very specific about
who will be held accountable, the exact due date, including
the time of day, and how "completion" will be measured.
Follow this rule throughout the entire process of converting goals into specific deliverables. Chart #8-2 takes the
goal of increasing revenues by $2.0M and breaks it into
more detailed deliverables.

Chart #8-2

Actual Work Product Converting Twelve Month Goals into Deliverables

Action Item	Accountability	Due Date	Measurement
Goal: Increase revenues by $2.0M	**Director of Sales partnering with Director of Marketing**		
Analyze current and last year sales by region and product line	Sales manager and each sales representative	10/1/xx 5:00p.m.	Sales report that analyzes product sales by region
Analyze current and last year sales by customer and product line	Sales manager and each sales representative	10/1/xx 5:00p.m.	Sales report that analyzes product sales by customer
Identify top customers that account for 80% of sales by region and product line	Sales manager and sales representatives	10/1/xx 5:00p.m.	Sales report of top customers
Create detailed sales account plans for top clients from step #3	Sales manager and sales representatives	10/1/xx 5:00 p.m.	Account plans for top clients

The Director of Sales and the Director of Marketing will take this document back to their sales organization and repeat the process of converting deliverables into more detailed action plans with action items and due dates as covered in more detail in chapter 9.

You will repeat the brainstorming and discussion of detailed action items for each of your strategic goals and their twelve month tactical objectives. You will repeat the process of prioritizing and consolidating action items into a table that maps out the deliverable, the responsible party, the due date, and the measurement of the deliverable.

Here is another example of actual work product from a strategic planning session where the executive team converted twelve month goals into deliverables with specific action items, who was responsible for completing the items, the specific due date, and the measurement of a successfully achieved deliverable. The examples below are based on a planning session for the year 2013 that was held during September 2012 with some of the work beginning immediately after the planning session so that my client had a head start on the upcoming year.

Increase gross margin in year one from 44 percent to 45 percent (from chart #8-1)

Responsible executive: Director of Manufacturing or Purchasing

Partner: Supply Chain Manager

Chart #8-3

Converting twelve Month Goals into Deliverables

Action Item	Accountability	Due Date	Measurement
Goal: Increase gross margin by 1%	Director of MFG partnering with Supply Chain Manager		
Decrease materials costs	Purchasing	1/1/13	Add .50% to gross margin run rate
Consolidate supply chain vendors for better pricing	Purchasing	10/15/12	List of top supplies. Develop meeting schedule to discuss pricing and discount policies
Create programs to decrease waste and customer returns	Purchasing	10/15/12	Training schedule with subject, dates and expected measureable improvements in performance and how those improvements will be tracked and reported
Decrease cost of labor per unit of production	Shop floor manager	1/1/13	Add .50% to gross margin run rate
Increase productivity with line improvements	Shop floor manager	1/1/13	Establish new units produced or shipped per day

The Director of Purchasing or Manufacturing will take this document back to their team and develop further details, action items, and due dates as covered in more detail in chapter 9.

Once you have completed the same steps for each of the year 1 tactical goals, each member of the executive team that is held accountable for the achievement of a goal will have a document that includes all of their goals and action items for the upcoming twelve month period. As I have shown in the prior examples, each goal should be broken down into smaller details by the entire executive team. Discussions about ideas and suggested solutions for every goal must contain input from every executive team member. At the end of each section of your strategic planning discussions, when you have completely reviewed the goals, you and your executive team must again test the reality of the created goals. Discuss whether or not you can reach your goals based upon the exchange of knowledge and discussions that you have had during your strategic planning session. Can the goals be achieved? What road blocks could occur and how should the company respond to any challenges?

By the time you and your team have concluded your discussions on the detailed goals you will have validated every goal you have set as well as created the tracking measurements and timelines that will guide your company through the implementation process.

The next step your team will complete at the strategic planning retreat is to create a communication plan that will inform 100 percent of the employees of the company about the outcome of the strategic planning session. The communication plan should include a general statement that all members of the executive team will present to their individual groups. Your strategic goals that were created utilizing the 1-3-5 Method of Goal Setting™ should be explained to all of your employees including the industry growth projections, the market share calculations, and the competitors' rankings for current year market share. In addition, each executive team member will have their detailed twelve month tactical objectives that they will review with their teams. Dates and timetables should be established in the communication plan so that all teams are meeting and completing their implementation plans within ten working days after the strategic planning retreat. I provide you with greater detail about the communication plan in chapter 9.

The momentum of the strategic planning retreat needs to be maintained once back at the office. The faster you are able to implement your plan for strategic alignment, the faster you will achieve your strategic goals. You and your executive team have taken the first steps in achieving strategic alignment. The next critical step in the process is driving the achievement of your strategic plans down through your organization so that 100 percent of your employees have two to three actions items to complete.

Checklist for converting goals into deliverables:

- Identify year one goals
- Identify who on the executive team will be accountable for the delivery of the year one goals

- Discuss each goal and create detailed action items
  - Create detailed lists of action items
  - Complete a detailed discussion of all the elements of a deliverable goal
  - Test the reality of your established goals

- Create a tracking document for each goal and its deliverables
- Communication plan and timetables for team meetings

NOTES:

CHAPTER 9:
IMPLEMENTING YOUR PLAN – DRIVING YOUR GOALS DOWN THE ORGANIZATION

> ➤ Communication to the whole organization
> ➤ Meeting with teams
> ➤ Discussion, creation, and delegation of tactical objectives
> ➤ Involve 100 percent of the employees of the company
> ➤ Examples of tracking documents

At the beginning of this book I stated that most strategic plans begin to fail within two weeks after the strategic planning session. You and your executive team can prevent this from happening to your organization by adhering to your implementation plan that involves detailed discussions and review with every team within your organization. The meetings that you and your executive team will have with your organization following your strategic planning retreat will get everyone involved in your efforts to harness the power of strategic alignment. Every employee will be given the opportunity to share their ideas and participate in discussions. Throughout this critical step in the strategic alignment process you are getting 100 percent of your employees to share in the responsibility of achieving your common goals. Through this process, your employees are empowered to create their own goals that correlate to your organization's goals. When employees are involved in creating their own action items and goals, they are more willing to accept the responsibility for reaching those goals. The result of this empowerment is that all of your employees take ownership of the goals that they helped create.

That's the power of strategic alignment.

Communication plan

Everyone in your company knows that you and the executive team have been out of the office creating a strategic plan. They want to know what you accomplished. Since you are relying on 100 percent of your employees to contribute to reaching your strategic goals, you must get everyone involved in the process. I recommend that you immediately (within twenty-four hours after you return to the office) have a short all-company meeting during which you briefly explain the goals you have created, why you have set them as your goals, and how every employee will contribute to the achievement of those goals. You should also explain that every employee will be involved in team meetings where the goals will be discussed in greater detail. All of your employees need to know that their individual contributions are critical to the company achieving its strategic goals. An all-company meeting demonstrates to everyone in your organization the importance that you place on achieving these goals and the vital role everyone plays.

Team Meetings - Converting Deliverables into Individual Employee Action Items

It is critical to your strategic alignment that your executive team convenes meetings within twenty-four to forty-eight hours after your all-company meeting. During those initial team meetings your executive team will discuss the process of involving 100 percent of your employees in the achievement of your twelve month tactical goals. During their first meeting, the team leader will review the basic goals and outcomes as delineated in the communication plan developed at the strategic planning retreat. Each strategic goal and twelve month tactical goal needs to be reviewed with each team so that 100 percent of the employees of your company understand the basis of each goal and the importance of the achievement of each goal. The employees should leave the first meeting with the objective of returning to the second meeting with their ideas on what they can do to help reach the twelve month tactical goals. During the second team meeting, all employee ideas should be reviewed and discussed. Once an employee's action items have been validated by the team as contributing to the achievement of the twelve month tactical goals, they should be added to the team's goal table as depicted in chart #9-1

During the team meeting, the team leader should maintain the same type of open dialogue that you had at the strategic planning retreat so that the meeting promotes creativity during the discussion of each tactical goal. Every team member should be asked specifically "What can you think of that will help the company achieve our goals?" Every participant needs to generate three individual activities that they will complete with deadlines and measurable outcomes. Each of those activities needs to be documented by the team leader and by the individual. As an example, in chapter 8 the following deliverables were created for the sales team:

Chart #9-1

Creating Individual Employee Action Items from Twelve Month Goals

Twelve Month Deliverable from the Strategic Planning Session

Action Item	Accountability	Due Date	Measurement
Goal: Increase revenues by $2.0M	Director of Sales partnering with Director of Marketing		
1. Create detailed sales account plans for top clients from step #3	Sales manager and sales representatives	10/1/xx 5:00 p.m.	Account plans on who will be buying what products from your current client list. Detailed selling plan on how sales will be obtained. Projected revenues that will meet current year sales goals.

Using the same format for creating and tracking deliverables the sales team would have each of the sales representatives complete a detailed deliverables tracking document that would specify the name of the client and the due date for completing their sales account plans with the resulting document looking like the one depicted in Chart #9-1.

The same level of detail needs to be accomplished by every executive team member with 100 percent of the employees in the company. Each employee should have a detailed tracking document like chart #9-1 that clearly defines their deliverables and expected timelines for each action item and a clearly identified outcome of the work they are to accomplish.

One of my client companies had set the goal of increasing their gross margin by 3 percent in the upcoming twelve month period. In the accounting department, the controller reviewed that goal with his accounting team. The accounts payable (AP) clerk assigned to vendors A-L identified a way that she could help improve gross margins. She knew that they were losing cash discounts because it was taking them too long to get invoices approved by the buyers. She and the other AP clerk (M-Z) created action items that included the following:

Chart #9-2

Deliverables and Tracking Document for AP Clerks

Action Item	Accountability	Due Date	Measurement
Develop a system for electronic approval by buyers of all invoices	AP clerk A-L partnering with AP clerk M-Z	10/15/ 5:00 p.m.	Decrease invoice approval process from 13 days to 6 days.
Process payments in time to get 100% of cash discounts available. Accomplish a run rate that will equate to the twelve month goal.	AP clerks A-Z	11/30/ 5:00 p.m.	Increase cash discounts for the upcoming twelve month period from $75,000 per year to $235,000 per year

This is a prime example of what can happen when you get everyone involved in helping achieve your goals. You never know where the next great idea will come from. Two accounts payable clerks identified what they could do to help reach the goal. In a subsequent follow-up with the controller for this company, I was told that the two clerks exceeded their goals. They created a new electronic invoice approval process that cut the approval time to less than five days. The purchasing department then began negotiating better cash discount terms with their vendors and negotiating cash discount terms with vendors that had never offered them before. This single deliverable created over $300,000 in added cash discounts in twelve months, and it started with one employee, an accounts payable clerk. This is an everyday example of the results that can be obtained by harnessing the power of strategic alignment to exceed your organization goals.

When each executive team leader completes this process of meeting with their teams and identifying specific action items for 100 percent of the employees on their teams, they must then review all of the items and confirm that they will help the entire company achieve its twelve month tactical goals. In my example, the Director of Sales needs to meet with the sales manager and add up the revenues that are forecasted in each of the sales representatives' sales account plans for current and targeted new clients. This will confirm that the sales plans will achieve the twelve month revenue goals. If the sales account plans do not meet the revenue goals then the sales manager needs to review the plans with each of the sales representatives in order to add more new business to their targeted new clients.

I worked with one company that completed the sales account planning process. Through that process they realized that their marketplace could not support the sales growth that they had projected for their twelve month goals. The sales director met with the CEO and they reconvened the executive team to quickly review the outcome of the sales account planning process. Their ultimate decision was to decrease their sales growth goals for the upcoming twelve month period. The new goals would still require that the sales team pushed itself to achieve its goals. The sales team felt empowered by the process because they could influence the goal setting process. They took complete ownership and responsibility for setting and reaching their goals. I reviewed the sales results with the CEO at the end of that twelve month period, and he told me that the sales team had worked smart and hard all year long, in a down economy, and managed to meet their sales goals. The CEO knew it was a mighty effort and he praised his sales team for holding themselves accountable for reaching their goals.

This same process of identifying detailed action items needs to be completed by each member of the executive team for all of their teams and 100 percent of your employees. Your executive team is to be held accountable for the delivery specific goals, and they need to verify that their teams' efforts will help them achieve those goals. Every employee must have two or three clearly defined deliverables that have a timeline and a measurable outcome. The magnitude of the combined effort of 100 percent of your employees becomes huge. If you have one hundred employees, your organization will have two hundred to three hundred individual deliverables in place that will help you exceed your goals. By focusing individual efforts on two to three specific deliverables, you are changing the way your organization works.

Everyone in the organization participates in the delivery of the company's strategic goals. They take ownership of their piece of the goal. Once each executive team member has validated that their team efforts will deliver all of their goals, they need to report to the executive team giving a detailed review on their team's strategic alignment and how their team will achieve their goals.

Mandatory follow up meetings
It is the responsibility of a strategic planning facilitator to hold you and your team accountable for leading your orga-

nization toward achieving its goals. Without mandatory meetings, organizations lose sight of the important work they completed during their strategic planning session and the importance of the executive team's consistent leadership that is required to achieve those goals.

As part of my engagement with clients, I require that they have four additional follow up meetings after the initial two-week review meeting (5 meetings total). In these meetings, which are scheduled every 45-60 days, I facilitate the executive team through a series of discussions: on the progress made, any successes to celebrate and identifying or assessing any additional resources which are required for deliverables that are lagging. If they need to respond to any external or internal changes, I lead them through their discussion and the creation of deliverable action items. Often during these meetings new action items will be created as a result of changes in operations or personnel, as well as the addition of new goals. During these meetings, the discussion should include what is trending in their industry and what is happening to their competitors.

Two week executive team plan review
The executive team should reconvene for a two to four hour strategic planning review meeting two weeks after the conclusion of their strategic planning session to review their detailed action plans, deliverables, and how their plans have aligned 100 percent of their team's efforts that will drive the company toward achieving 100 percent of its twelve month goals. During this review session, your calendar of meetings for continual follow-up must be established.

Most of my clients have weekly executive team meetings. They review their progress on their strategic initiatives. They complete their strategic plan updates within the first ten to fifteen minutes of the meeting. Their discussions include progress made, challenges to completing their deliverables within their detailed timetables, and requests for assistance or guidance from the rest of the executive team.

Your entire executive committee should reconvene for two to three hours for a quarterly strategic plan review. This meeting should include a review and update on all twelve month goals, progress, challenges, and, possibly, revisions of goals. The quarterly plan review should follow the format and agenda of the strategic planning retreat. For your first quarterly plan review meeting, your strategic planning facilitator should preside over the meeting to insure that your quarterly plan review session is open and the creative communications process becomes a regular part of the meeting environment.

Each team leader should celebrate the successes of his team's accomplishments. Those celebrations should include individual recognition for employees who have achieved goals. The celebration of success should be held frequently. In one client's office they had a recognition and congratulations celebration every two weeks where individual employees were spotlighted and praised for their achievements by their team leader and by the CEO. I personally believe that one of the most powerful forms of employee recognition is a public thank you from the CEO.

Checklist for implementing your plan:

- Communicate strategic goals to all teams in an all-company meeting
- Hold team meetings within twenty-four to forty-eight hours after the all-company meeting
- Develop team and individual deliverables
- Validate goals through detailed deliverables
  - Every employee contributes with their deliverables
- Report back to the executive team on deliverables
- Celebrate the successes
- Schedule and hold mandatory quarterly plan reviews with your executive team

NOTES:

CHAPTER 10:
WHY STRATEGIC PLANS FAIL

> ➢ Exposed Accountability
> ➢ 20/60/20 Rule
>   a. The coaching and culling process
> ➢ Leadership

Exposed Accountability

Exposed accountability changes the way an organization works by creating clearly defined goals that are converted into measurable deliverables with date specific timelines, all of which are subjected to continuous follow-up. Your executive team and all of their teams formulate their own deliverables with clearly defined measurements and due dates. The frequency of review and reporting on progress toward goal achievement provides the transparency. You should have weekly executive team meetings that include as the first item on the agenda a review and status report on tactical objectives including any progress or lack of progress toward achieving the goals. Weekly or bi-weekly meetings held by your team leaders and their members should also include as their first agenda item a review of progress made toward tactical objectives. If one of your executives has a one on one meeting with someone on their team or if you have a one on one meeting with an executive team member, you need to include the tactical objective review and update as the first item on your agenda. Continuous review creates transparency, which results in exposed accountability.

The consistent review of goals is mandatory if an organization wants to achieve strategic alignment. If a team or an individual is on track to meet its goals, they should be praised. Success must be celebrated. If teams or individuals are not on track to meet their goals, they need to be challenged and coached so that they can meet their goals on time. The concept of exposed accountability can create both excitement and fear in people. Being held accountable can inspire them to meet their goals or drive them to fight the process, blame circumstances, or fault other people.

I worked with a company where one member of the executive team had been promoted beyond his capabilities and experience. The executive team left their strategic planning session with a set of deliverables. It became obvious very quickly that this executive was having difficulty in getting his team organized around its goals and deliverables. The first due date for the strategic plan review came two weeks after the planning retreat. This executive came to that meeting with very little accomplished. The CEO held a private meeting with that individual and offered him coaching to see if he could develop into a better team leader. Within a short period of time, the individual and the CEO came to a mutual agreement that the leadership role at the firm was beyond the individual's ability and work experience. The CEO determined that there was a better role for him to perform elsewhere in the firm. The rest of the executive team responded well to the personnel change. They had been concerned about the fact that critical parts of the strategic goals were not being completed which would limit the success of their work and the company's ability to achieve its strategic goals.

You will find that some of your employees do not like exposed accountability, because it reveals that they may not have the ability or experience to complete their deliverables and achieve their goals. Some of those employees will respond to coaching and mentoring. You and your executive team can help them by sharing your experience and giving them guidance when they have problems completing their action items. If they are unable to meet their commitments and their portion of the strategic goals, then you need to make a change or they will derail or delay your progress toward achieving your strategic goals. Having someone in your organization that is not successfully achieving their goals will become a distraction for the rest of the employees and will become a negative influence on everyone's commitment to achieving their goals. I have seen this many times where other employees will wonder why they should be working diligently on achieving their goals when someone else in the organization is allowed to not meet their time commitments for completing their action items. Immediate action needs to be taken when someone is not delivering their goals. If you don't take decisive action your momentum toward reaching your strategic goals will be slowed or even stopped. In fact, most people work better when they have clearly defined deliverables that will lead them to achieving their goals.

It makes their work easier. They have no question as to what they are supposed to accomplish and when they are to have their tasks completed.

You will find that some people will sabotage the process because they are fearful of being held accountable for not be able to reach their goals. You may discover that members of your executive team fear exposed accountability, and they will try to derail your goal of becoming a strategically aligned organization. Some of the tactics that I have seen people use to block the alignment process from becoming successful include:

They don't participate in discussions during the strategy session or during your follow-up meetings. They usually sit in the meetings looking totally distracted or with their arms crossed in a defiant pose.

The only comments they will make during meetings are negative comments. They only point out problems and never offer solutions.

They make side comments that disparage the process like: "These things never work. These meetings just create more paperwork."

They constantly bad-mouth the strategic alignment efforts as being a waste of time.

They make excuses for not completing their steps in the strategic alignment process, i.e., "I didn't have time to get the task done because I was too busy doing my job." (That's an actual quote from an executive team member.)

They won't help other members of the executive team complete their partnered deliverables. They do this by postponing meetings or not delivering their actions items on time.

They don't attend the weekly executive meetings or are always late to any meeting that involves reporting on their activities toward achieving their deliverables.

I am quite certain that you have people like this on your teams. These are very common characteristics that I see in every organization. CEOs are fortunate if they do not have these non-performers on their executive team. It's more common than not to have one. Afraid of failure, weaker employees fear the transparency of this strategic alignment process and recognize that it will reveal their inability to get their job done right.

20-60-20 Rule

In the change management and human resources world, there is a commonly used evaluation that is referred to as the "20-60-20 rule." I use the 20-60-20 rule to clarify to the executive team and the CEO that they will encounter resistance and acceptance as they try to implement strategic alignment. The way that I apply the 20-60-20 rule to the process of strategic alignment is that 20 percent of the people in your organization will be champions of the strategic alignment process. They love it, and they will fight to make it successful. 60 percent of your people will respect the process, and they will get their part done because it is their job. The final 20 percent will fight the process because they don't like change or they don't want a spotlight (exposed accountability) shining on their inability to get their job done.

One of my clients was discussing his team with me during a meeting held after his strategy retreat. One executive member was just not getting the job done like the rest of the executive team. I reminded the CEO of the 20-60-20 rule, and I could see in his eyes the realization that the 20-60-20 rule had to be applied to 100 percent of his employees including his executive team. He had the wrong person heading up that team.

The most successful way to achieve strategic alignment is to make sure your champions (top 20 percent) are focusing their efforts on the middle (60 percent) people. It is the largest part of your team, and they must stay focused on the achievement of their goals. You, as the company leader, have to focus on your bottom 20 percent, especially since the rule includes your executive team. You need to coach or cull the executive team members who are not working to help achieve strategic alignment of your resources. A negative attitude on your executive team or, for that matter, on any of your teams, will influence the desire and attitude of the other members of the team. The detractors must be guided to achieving their goals through coaching and consistent affirmation that strategic alignment will occur with them or without them. If they cannot make the change, then you or your team leaders have to get them out of the organization so that they cannot continue to stand in the way of your efforts to reform your organization into a team of achievers.

I recommend that my clients evaluate their employees on the basis of capability and capacity. If they are capable of getting the work done but have too much to complete, then they have a capacity problem and may need additional resources to help them deliver their responsibilities. If they have the capacity and enough time to get their job function completed, but are unable to complete the work, then they lack in capability. You can try to expand their capability by coaching or giving them additional training. If they still cannot complete their job function, then you will be required to either put them into another job function or ask them to leave your organization.

Leadership
It is vital to the successful achievement of the strategic goals that you, the leader of the entire organization, stay fully committed and overtly vocal about your continued belief in strategic alignment. The successful implementation of a strategic plan and driving strategic alignment down through your organization takes powerful leadership. You, as the leader of your organization, need to demonstrate your commitment to the process by consistently asking about your team's progress toward successfully completing deliverables. The best way to display your commitment is to always start your meetings with a discussion of an individual's progress or a team's progress toward achieving their goals. Ask if there are any resources that they need or if they need assistance from other executive team members.

Every leader also needs to be involved in the recognition and celebration of successes. One of the divisions inside a company that I worked with would gather their whole team together every two to three weeks for a quick fifteen minute progress report and acknowledgement of any deliverables they had achieved. The leader of the team always included the entire executive team as a demonstration of the company's commitment to the achievement of the strategic goals and to the importance of recognizing and celebrating an individual's completion of a deliverable. The employees that had completed a deliverable where recognized during the meeting with a lot of whooping and clapping. Those employees told me that it was a proud moment for them because they received recognition for their accomplishments and a personal thank you from their CEO. Following each quarterly plan review by the executive committee there should be a company-wide update of the progress being made toward achieving your strategic goals. That communication can be done with a broadcast email, a newsletter with the updated progress report, a very quick general meeting of the entire company, or by holding team meetings where the progress report is reviewed and discussed.

You and your executives must demonstrate through your actions that you are committed to the achievement of your strategic plan goals. That will keep the attention and momentum of your organization focused on those goals and the deliverables that need to be delivered in order for your organization to achieve your goals. It will take committed leadership from you and your executive team to harness the power of strategic alignment in your organization.

Checklist for how to prevent strategic plan failure:

- Identify the champions

- Identify the detractors

- Organize the champions to provide leadership

- Evaluate capability versus capacity

- Coach or cull the detractors

- Provide continuous, committed leadership

- Celebrate the successes

- Communicate progress toward achieving strategic goals

NOTES:

CHAPTER 11: HARNESSING THE POWER OF STRATEGIC ALIGNMENT

Strategic alignment is hard work but the rewards are huge. This book has taken you and your executive team through the preparation for and completion of a truly great strategic planning session. The strategic plan and the tactical twelve month objectives that you created will serve as a blueprint for achieving your strategic goals. Using your strategic plan as your focal point, you and your executive team have started to drive strategic alignment down through your organization by getting 100 percent of your employees to focus their efforts on exceeding your organization's goals. You cannot make the assumption that everyone will do their part just because you and your executive team have created clearly defined strategic goals. You and your executive team need to manage your entire company through the process of driving strategic alignment down through your organization. It also requires that your executive team confirms that each employee's goals and deliverables correlate with your strategic goals.

While I was writing this book, I met with a company that was frustrated by the fact that they were unable to achieve the goals that they had created during their strategic planning retreats for each of the preceding two years. In both planning sessions, their executive team had completed intelligent work including creating clearly defined and achievable goals. When they returned to their office from each planning retreat, they told the rest of the organization about the strategic goals they had created. Their plans began to fail from that point forward. They were unable to achieve their goals because they did not work closely with their teams as they went through the process of clearly defining individual employee deliverables. The outcome was that each team came up with ideas, action items, and deliverables that had no relationship to the goals that were created by the executive team at the planning session. The teams and individuals had failed to align their goals with the strategic goals of the company. Coupling that with the fact that the executive team did not have a consistent program for communication and followup meetings caused the organization to fail to achieve its strategic goals for two consecutive years.

Every level of the process of driving goal alignment and goal achievement down through your organization requires a focused and determined effort from you and your executive team. You and your executive team must continuously confirm that 100 percent of your organization is working on deliverable action items that will lead to achieving your goals. Strategic alignment of individual goals throughout all of your employees will change the way your organization works. Your reward for your hard work, the hard work of your executive team, and the hard work of all of your employees will be watching your organization consistently exceed its goals.

Share this book with your executive team and other key employees so that they too will be able to learn about what it takes to harness the power of strategic alignment. In preparation for your planning retreat, pass this book around to your executive team in order to maximize their understanding of the strategic alignment process and what you expect to achieve during your upcoming strategic planning retreat.

Get started immediately on implementing strategic alignment in your organization. The sooner you get started, the sooner that day will come when you walk into your office knowing that 100 percent of your employees are working to achieve your strategic goals.

With your commitment and leadership, you can harness the power of strategic alignment and exceed your organization's goals.

NOTES:

APPENDIX

Strategic Alignment Process diagram

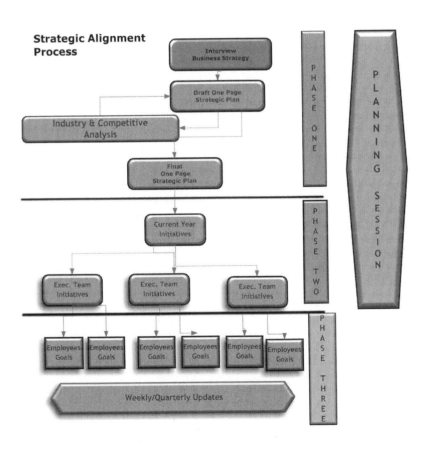

Strategically Aligned Organization

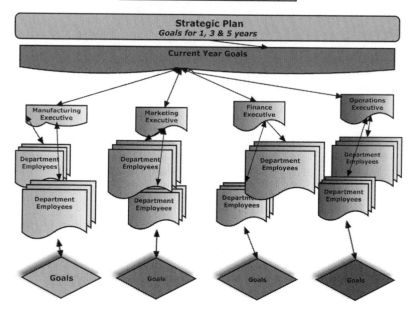

FORMS AND TEMPLATES

Go to my website and create a login using your email address as your username. This will give you access to the "Article" section of my website where you can download sample forms. In the future, when you enter my website you will enter your email address in the upper right-hand corner of my home page for all future logins to gain access to these forms and templates.

Sample forms and templates found on my website:
Objective/initiative tracking forms

Sales account plans

One page strategic plan
Go to http://www.gazelles.com/ for information and free downloads on the One Page Strategic Plan